Even the
Saints Audition

Even the Saints Audition

Poems

Rachel "Raych" Jackson

Published by Button Poetry / Exploding Pinecone Press
Minneapolis, MN 55403 | http://www.buttonpoetry.com

—

Cover design: Hector Padilla

ISBN - 978-1-943735-62-4

For my family & fellow church babies

Contents

To God be the Glory
To God be the Glory
To God be the Glory
for the things He has done.
—Andraé Crouch

Whole time she is a church girl,
so it's a blessing.
—P. RICO

Even the
Saints Audition

On Job
A retelling

At dinner, God brags about his best saint. Job[1] is God's most loyal follower. He prays on time & worships loud with his head down. A role model; blessed & rich. The Devil picks at his plate quietly. He doesn't like his greens leaking onto the cornbread; God hands him an extra plate without the request. The Devil lays his challenge on the table in between steaming dishes. *Prove it.* Without blessings Job's faith will weaken. Like Moses, like Samson, like every human who confuses an anointing with absolution. *Remove your protection & Job will curse you.* With the Devil's help, anyone will betray God. Like Adam, like David, like every human who confuses being a favorite with safety. God lent Job to him; Job was His anyway. The Devil shouldn't dare God in His own house & not expect follow through.

1. pronounced [Jōb]

Job nailed the part;   praised God the whole scene.
        after all he owned was destroyed
                after his children were murdered
        after pus filled sores littered his body

God let the Devil   experiment
        until scraps & bones
                lay on both their plates.
        He proved His point on a full stomach.

                You win God.

At the end of the night   God dropped
        extra blessings on Job while packing
                the Devil a to go bag.
        Separate containers of course,

he hates his food touching
                more than losing a bet.

                We'll have to do this again sometime.

Who else is worthy?

& that's how the story

goes, the Devil & God

having dinner & a show.

My Sunday School teacher

claims this is a lesson about

faith during the hard times.

God will reward us for

suffering. I peel through

each chapter at home &

the scab gets worse.

I return to the Devil asking

permission to torment.

I can't overlook God saying *yes*.

Act One

On Job

God will give you nothing more than you can bear
    is the rehearsed mantra. It's drilled on
    the inside wrist of every person in my
    momma's church. Their skin has already
    healed around the screw, convincing them
    abuse is necessary in relationships.

God will give you nothing more than you
    keeps the saints hungry for the reward
    after. They bob in the church's nest with
    their mouths wide open & try to snatch
    encouragement from the pulpit.

God will give you nothing more
    The Sunday School teacher cuts her fingers
    collecting rusted grace from the prayer.
    There's a new test in class; an undeveloped
    saint blooming with questions. The choir
    director should be ashamed. A mother who
    raises a sinner is no mother at all.

God will give you nothing
    The Sunday School teacher reports her
    day to God & waits on the edge of her bed.
    She stretches her neck up & caws for an
    answer. God has to bless her for teaching a
    child whose soul is already lost.

I ask *Where do children go when they die?* in Sunday School

This class grooms me to be a good
Christian. I learn to dress modest.
I cover my body from the shoulders
to the knees & wait to go to heaven.
In Sunday School I ask if hell
has an age requirement. Here, I'm
a *unique blessing.* My Sunday School

teacher announces how grateful she is
for me in a meeting with my mom.
She reminds her Eve was also a curious
woman, who God cursed. The next week
I ask why God kills kids. The next week
we're in another meeting. I'm not satisfied
with filling gaps in the scripture

with a faith that is not mine. Years later I am
at another baby's funeral, sitting on the
wrong side. I want to teach the audience
what I know. I've been a jealous expert
for years. The correct way to sit is upright.
I know not to look at the rest of the amateurs
here. I understand the casket is the size of

a toy box before the service. I understand
the preacher will fill his empty eulogy
with words like *God's plan* & *sacrifice.*
This funeral is any other lesson until the
baby's photo giggles from the obituary, until
only one pall bearer's name steps forward to lift,
until I blink & am gliding down I-57 failing
to drown my own envy weighing down this pedal.

I ask *What does circumcision mean?* in Sunday School

Remnants of sex dreams run
through my ears. They pitter patter
in my head during every service

while my dress is sewn to the pew
seat cushion. I'm trapped here,
in the front & piano side trying

to shake the filth out in disguise
of praise hands & holy worship.
In this church I'm the valuable

section in the snow that's never
touched. I'm waiting to be melted
away by marriage— marriage only.

In church I want nothing more
than a handprint on me. Church
mothers teach my lower region is

a frozen wasteland. *Nothing the Lord
is proud of can grow from such a void.*
I don't mind the frigid temperatures.

I'm my best company. My body is
my temple, I keep it tidy when I visit.
I appreciate my fingers more

than older women flipping through
Hymnals until they find the right spot
for their song. I stay in tuned with

my fingers. Make sure the key is not
too sharp. Don't want anyone to hear
me explore my new found melody

that lulls me to sleep each night. It feels
like satin. Soft, like I knew it was. I create
mosaics in the lonely winters. Snow angels

mastering the devil's dance. My fingertips
are coated with glitter now. A sparkling
layer reminding me how evil I must be.

Keep my nails short & continue to
groom the eager monster that gnaws
down there. Consuming under the slightest

panty rub & drafts up my dress. Suffocate
it under tights, skirts & gospel songs
praising a young woman who stays true

to her virtue. A young woman whose value
depends on how pure she is, how cold she is.
A girl with a sex eroded mind; the uneven

edges are lined with lust & craving. It's better
for me to pretend my insides are empty
rooms in the Lord's house. Can't let them

know there's a leak in my basement
during the week. I cross my legs tight
at the knees & pray the urge dies. I know

I'm not in control anymore. Oh, how I
yearn to be alone with my hands.

Praying in terror

Terror is a sinner's uniform. All my panic attacks
are a couple sizes too big. Forgotten hand-me-downs.

The first public panic attack is at church camp surrounded
by saints who believe terror is what a sinner deserves.

Some saints pray the spirit out. Some saints pray I stop
faking. Every word is coherent. I don't understand them.

A group of adults praying over a child who can't
breathe. If God listened to sinners I would've

prayed my mind right a long time ago. Shortly after,
I was baptized by my own choice. How can I show

God I'm committed without practicing to drown?
I'm performing for a spot in heaven. All my commitments

are public & won't last. Some saints pray the spirit in.
Some saints pray I stop faking. I earned my place

in the prayer circle. I thank God & he guides me
back to having my attacks in private.

Church Girl answers *what is sadness?*

sadness is a wolf. you could think you've
built everything strong but with a *woosh,*
sadness can huff & puff & blow all that
happy down. then your other feelings eat

you. you can hide him too. save sadness
for later. a secret pet I let escape. even when
I'm happy it stays behind me. if you
don't lock your windows at night

sadness can creep in & lay next to you.
he gets so big when it's just us. believes
in himself. I'm never alone. my feet are
sadness' feet. we walk places together

like friends, but I know we're not friends.
friends don't need me to hate myself.
I know what sadness is. I know my adults
don't point at him in the room. we call

every funeral a *homegoing.* my mom clapped
in the choir when her best friend died. we
sing loudly over sadness. close my eyes
tight when we try to pray it away. I see

him the most here. I'm the only one
who stares back in class. My Sunday
School teacher says when I'm saved God will
keep me happy. *Depression is a punishment;*

a sickness for sinners. we learn what she wants.
when she passes out our Bibles I pretend not
to see how she moves through the room;
walking around sadness whispering *excuse me.*

Come Thou Fount Hymn

An erasure

Come,
Tune my heart to
Stream
      songs
Teach me
Sung   above
      the mount, I'm fixed upon it
Mount of Thy   love

Oh,   how great a debt
Daily I'm constrained to
Let
      my   heart
        wander, Lord,
                I love
       my heart,   take and seal it
       for Thy courts above

A good saint worships & sacrifices

My dad sings in roars. Shows off the rotten

tooth dotting his smile from the stage. He howls

beneath the pulpit. A good saint worships

& sacrifices. Back pain reclaims him

on the ride home. We can't help him out the

car. Instead we fling our hollow prayers on

top of his groans. Thank God first & loudly.

We make joy our redundant noise. Tonight

he led our congregation in praise. Now,

I walk behind him up the stairs; my hands,

a sturdy brace he won't buy. At the top

step another howl escapes. Who is this

wailing beast in my home? He sits & hums;

his once loud roar now a simple whimper.

I thank the church for blessing my mother's womb

All of my friends are dying. I'm competitive
at their funerals; sit in front & think
                    I could have died first.
I read *be grateful* in every Scripture
& thank God for my life as a sinner.
                    I am a sinner with no life.
Each breath, a stagnant celebration. I excuse myself
from new people to take my birth control on time.
        The pill bounces
down my throat in familiar jabs. I don't hold babies
& want to cry inside her again. Living
                has proved to be a challenge
I am ready to back down from. When I lay
in her bed she counts my fingers & toes
                between sentences. & glosses
over the memory of the doctor's suggestion.
You're my miracle baby. Her words wind through
                the night prayer
until I know I can hang up the phone.
I've decided yesterday I want children.
        I'll decide tomorrow no one deserves
this world. On a good day I read a pro-life
advertisement that *prays for the sinners*
                & thank God for my mom's faith.
I try to thank God she didn't backslide.
On a bad day I can't decide if I should thank God
                or His guilt.

Touching

My mom says I follow
her *like a germ* without knowing
    my mind is infected.
We laugh.
I hover in the kitchen
like a cough stuck in her throat.
    At Thanksgiving,
I over salt the greens & get
demoted to the dishes. I'm the glass
    that needs polishing.
Know the constant rub will
      make it clean.

//

At Tuesday night service I find I don't need
to touch myself to *touch myself*. I can toy
with my muscles while smiling in a pew.

A pulsing preteen heap pretending
to not think about how people in this church
were created. The Bible says Adam *knew* Eve

& she birthed Cain. Maya's parents
folded into each other like our tithing
envelopes. She's singing a hymn next to me.

I accidentally found my parents' condoms
yesterday. They can't afford another sinner.

//

I'm so neat.

I'm so careful.

Chores scrub

the secret until

my desire is blank.

I erase the dirt

in my head

    while vacuuming

    the living room.

    Stains yell

    the sins from

    my underwear.

    I wash a load

    for my family

    all by myself.

//

I cut my nails to be productive;
        need push the buttons on the machines easier.
My panties are smothered
        in the bottom of the hamper with dried flakes in the seat.
I'm so dirty. I'm so independent.
        Know how to work around what's broken.
I lay our clothes on the couches
        to dry while the dishes soak in hot water. I tell my mom
the laundry mat has a working dryer.
        Need to hide the extra drawers covering the arm rests.

//

These are adult feelings. No one teaches how
to feel before the blood. I'm told my body
is not built for lust. I am not a woman yet

but I want to be. An erupting girl who doesn't
track a cycle but ruins cotton panties. Shay taught
me how to pop my ass in the church bathroom

while our moms were upstairs in choir rehearsal.
I'm ready to grind on the nearest boy at school
the next day. I must be the only one who craves.

I want to ask my Sunday School teacher
if I will go to hell. How much am I sinning
when I'm only pleasuring myself?

//

The bathroom is the only door

I'm allowed to lock in this house.

I point out the ring around the toilet

while gripping Ajax by the neck.

> My mom's impressed at my surge of housework.
>
> *Cleanliness is next to Godliness.* I'll be a good wife.
>
> Suppression is next to salvation. I'll be a good
>
> sinner. I turn the latch & clean myself of the
>
> *thoughts.* After, I run water to soak up the sound
>
> of crying. For now I only need myself.
>
> For now I only need my need.

Wasted grooming

The second man I try to have sex with gave me head like a shy frog trying to catch a fly. Hidden behind the neatly trimmed grass (if I do say so myself) but too nervous to make contact. Very wild & very apologetic. As much as I wanted to stop him somethings are too horrible to look away from! A car crash right through Sex Ed. Unsure of where to finally park, so it was more of a ramming of sorts. His tongue, a winding pink sloth missing each mark. He even let me turn on & watch Martin during. Somehow that wasn't a clue. The ceiling couldn't have been more entertaining. The creases & folds & paints chips all watching me not even pretend to be revved up. He smashed his tongue places like an ambitious hot wire begging for some type of spark & looked like an inexperienced mechanic under my hood. I shaved my ass for this?! Do you know how hard it is to find & snatch out the long curly hair? The blade is my metal predator but the prey finds strength in bushy numbers. This morning I was contorted in my shower like a cramped up mannequin. Ran my hand over the hard to reach spots for the Spike Test™ until I'm an eight ball. All this, for an orgasm I wrote on my to do list. After I stopped his imitation of an off beat harmonica player, I reached out my fist for a dap. I didn't want to be rude & offer a handshake. I feel like a dap has more of a commorodory tone to it. It's a solid gesture that says *Sir, I still fuck with you as a person but your head game is trash.* I only want to be with people that compliment how smooth my ass crack is that day. Need to find someone to appreciate this landing strip before my grade A sculpting becomes stubby.

Church Girls sing for the congregation

In between verses   Kia mentions   she's not pregnant anymore.

We start the second   verse. Polished   voices match each word.

Don't need   eye contact to harmonize.   Focus on parts

the audience   will erupt in praise at.   In fifteen minutes

we sing in front of   saints.   Why dwell on

disappeared sin?   Church Girls tilt far from   what they know

& snap back.   Purity is   an opinion.

We perform   the empty promise.   I ask about the dad.

We finish practice   with enough time   & plan to meet his friends.

Blue Ribbon

At first, an artist who loathes her work won't
throw it away. She'll stare at it on the shelf

to remind her of the time wasted. Even useless
decorations deserve a bit of shine. A snow globe

collecting dust, a forgotten picture on the desk,
a dirty token from the arcade, our first date.

I admired his wailing - his sorrow bounces
off the walls of my room. He didn't even murmur

when I dug my nails into his back, desperately carving
into someone who won't show our title. Instead,

he galloped to the mirror after. A proud horse
tracing each scar trail with his fingertips. Gnawed

his chin in a shoulder to marvel at my work.
I rip him up so well. I re-stitch him even better.

All of my art betrays me. All of my art leaves
without asking permission. This is the last night

I'll sleep next to unwanted edits. He rests to prepare
for his daily race in between women, oblivious I cut the reigns.

He'll forgive you again

If your relationship is as inconsistent as the radio
driving under viaducts on the way to his house,

it's not cheating. All exhales carry the same notes if your
eyes are closed. Moan lies, drawn out lies. Convince him

he's the one responsible for your swell. He cannot
contain you either. Even his shadow looks the same.

A smudge shaped him scrapes the wall in a familiar
motion. You lie on your back & trace the edges

with your thumb. Pray the outline stays until the
morning. At least that way he'll spend the night again

I sleep next to ███████████ **after**

When he holds me in his sleep
    I am a spider trapped under a glass jar.
Frantic because I can't move
    but so grateful he hasn't crushed me
        yet.

Act Two

On Job

What if
I feel
like Job
all
the
time?
My soul
an ant
running
through
God's fingers
trying
to find
stability
in a palm
already
pressed
against
the Devil's.

Even my nails hurt me

My nails fall in love with everything but
my hands. They commit to slammed doors

& cracks in the couch. Quietly rip themselves
from my fingers while my blood makes

the sound. I try to keep my nails on
my fingers with super glue & enlist keys

to pry open pop cans. Changed the shape
my nails naturally grow into. I am their sun.

Shaved the sides of their heads. I am
their shadow. Still, they want out. Even

when I tend to their needs before mine.
I dress my nails in glitter without asking

& paint them the color I deserve to feel. No
costume can make them belong to me. I hoped

they'd miss me. Instead, they giggle under
dust piles with my skin attached to their backs.

Mauled plastic chunks hiding in corners
of my apartment thrilled to be free.

from the Broken Fingernail

It must be nice
    to always be a part of the family
& to never question if your presence
    is welcome. I am a rotating disappointment,
a peaceful tune until the record scrape.
    Trying to make you see the beauty
in the jagged, the rich dirt as gold. Dare
    I compare myself to gold? I don't
have anyone who claims me as family.
    No one is praised for being jagged.
Even a sword is smooth on its sides
    & still welcome. Despite the cut,
despite the scrape. Why would I get
    used to being a disappointment?
Snatch a layer of gel over myself
    to hide the scrape. When I'm perfect
again, I will be accepted by my family.
    Only beings that look the same on
these hands can be welcome. Shine me
    until I am sparkling gold. Mold my parts
& create a family. Finally, I can have
    results from the scrape. Rub myself
against the hand so she too can feel
    the jagged. Wonder if the pain is always
worth the family? What happens if
    you can't reshape disappointment?
Throw the acetone on what pretends
    to be gold & watch the beauty burn away
with the welcome. After the appointment
    she always shows off what is no longer

jagged. Effortless hand motions cutting
    through the disappointment. If her hand
waves fast enough in the blur, we might all look like family.

"Fairytales do not tell children that the dragons exist. Children already know that dragons exist. Fairytales tell the children that the dragons can be killed."—GK Chesterton

Dragon

we build bunk beds / out of couches / stack cousins / on
brothers / on nieces / leather from the couch's seats / forces /
your cheek to be smooth / it's a lullaby / massages faces & ears
/ drowns out stampedes / of search parties / looking for your
mother / under the nearest crack rock / there's a vein on your
ankle / puffing / its chest out for attention / we all have one
/ royal blue / hidden entryways / elevate our fathers' thrones
/ even higher / parading / the insides of our elbows / during
family reunions / no need for long sleeves / admire the crevices
/ between our toes / play games with us / hide & seek / with
track marks / hot potato / with relative's couches / force your
cheek smooth / we welcome cloaked addiction / it's the thread
that sews us together / without it / we'd be separated / exposed
/ strung out / Monster / I know where you hide / syringes
give you neck cramps / instead / spread your wings / over well
groomed adults / & silent children / littered with blisters / from
mopping / their mother's faceprints off the floor / why do you
need / your ~~metal~~ spoon so much? / it's family dinner time / put
photos up over the reminders / bedtime stories / for the couch /
long tales / rock you to sleep / I'm sorry you believe us / practice
fairytales / about killing dragons / winged narratives / circling
exactly how she died /

Granny's wall

I'm glad we're up here. We're able to look down on her still & continue tradition.

How can you claim you miss me? You don't even remember my name.

Only put up photos of us smiling. They should remember we were happy.

She keeps wiping the glass above my face as if a rag will keep me clean.

Please keep the lights on I don't want to be alone with them in the dark.

I'll watch you fade. Bang my fists on the inside of all her picture frames.

An old photo

I only recognize my smile. My
elbow bone almost splits skin.
Misery is a funny secret. I'm sure

that's what I'm laughing about
in the picture; how I can shrink
in front of friends but swell

with compliments. Who'll pray
for me before I'm all gone? In
church, I learned to stop eating

when I want something from God.
Fasting shows devotion. I am ready
to be happy despite the hunger.

Small. Bad at taking up my own space.
Technically, a skeleton has great
bone structure. High cheekbones,

always smiling or at least showing
familiar teeth. My body fades &
the picture stays the same. I remember

that dress. I wasn't able to fit it
last year. Almost threw it away.

On Job

My momma's church would rather
blame depression   on the devil

as if they don't teach the story of Job,
          where God
          gambled a man's soul

& collected   the winnings
when he was done.

As if we can't feel the Devil
writhe under our skin already.

Don't you know
I know   it's the devil?

Why wouldn't I
be able to recognize him   by now?

Church Girl defends her hair cut

I remind them Samson was weak
well before his cut. Set his strength

in fragile strands. Faith that strong
is bound to leave you chopped.

Got the whole world convincing you
I need more. Contorted Rapunzel,

eager to walk in storms now. Bald
Weeping Willow—still a decoration.

Still bite & roar laced with neck roll.
Ain't a lion still a lion without his mane?

ode to the bald spots above my ears

I never asked for them, obviously.
Pools of smooth skin.   Open spaces
shining from the grease.   I brush my hair
quicker. My   bald spots make it easier
for me to slide on my glasses. I smothered them
under curtains of perms & braids. Told them
it was their fault everyone picks on me at school.
My poor,   undeserving splotches,
formed by my mother's   desperate
fingers. Can't rip out   beauty from the knaps,
beauty   is the knaps. Every crooked-tooth
comb that tore through the clusters is dead to me.
Resilient blotches will always   live on.
Have more room to settle. A country   pulled
out of the unwanted. My fashionable traumas.
Glinting   battle wounds I show off now.
Proof of all I had to take to *be acceptable.*
Tombstones set above each ear to mark
where my hair was mangled & uprooted.
        An anthem I always hear.

I see my bully a decade later

This bar is the empty hallway
& I'm an *ugly bitch* again. I keep
my head up when I notice I'm
caught in his eyeline. If I look down

he's already won. Back to being
the hairy girl whose skirts stretch
pass her knees. The girl who doesn't
understand her own religion. I know

how he'll look in the next decade.
Memorized his features in my nightmares
The song changes & he doesn't
recognize my face; the usual battle.

I've borrowed my mom's angel
for the night. Earlier today I admitted
I'm going to a party & she gave me
the loan for free. My mom says I'm pretty

but still teaches me to fight. My bully
says I'm pretty but keeps a closed fist
around his money. Time is rumored to
heal all wounds, no one claims it erases them.

When he leans in I jump & hold my cry
until I get home; a skill he's helped me
practice. I'm still me. I'm still me. I'm
my happiest alone, only have to fight myself.

For the black girl who doesn't know how to braid hair

Your hands have no more worth than tree stumps at harvest. Don't sit on my porch while I make myself useful. Braid secrets in scalps on summer days for my sisters. Secure every strand of gossip with tight rubber bands of value. What possessed you to ever grow your nails so long? How can you have history without braids?

A black girl is happiest when rooted to the scalp are braids. She dances with them whipping down her back like corn in winds of harvest. Braiding forces our reunions to be like the shifts your mothers work, long. I find that being surrounded by only your own is more useful. Gives our mixed blood more value. Solidifies your place with your race, with your sisters.

Your block is a layered cake of your sisters. Forced your lips quiet and sweet and they'll speak when they need to practice braids. Your hair length is the only part of you that holds value. The tallest crop is worshipped at harvest. So many little hands in your head. You are finally useful. Your hair is yours, your hair is theirs, your hair is, for a black girl, long.

Tender headed ass won't last 'round here long. Cut your nails and use your fists to protect yourself against your sisters. Somehow mold those hands useful. You hair won't get pulled in fights if they are in braids. Beat out the weak parts of the crops during harvest. When they are limp and without soul they have value.

If you won't braid or defend yourself what is your value? Sitting on the porch until dark sweeps in needing to be invited, you'll be needing long. When the crop is already used what is its worth after harvest? You'll learn that you can't ever trust those quick to call themselves your sisters. They yearn for the gold that is your braids. You hold on your shoulders a coveted item that is useful.

Your presence will someday become useful. One day the rest of your body will stagger under the weight of its value. Until then, sit in silence in the front with your scalp on fire from the braids. I promise you won't need anyone too long. Soon you will love yourself on your own, without the validation of sisters. No longer a stump wailing for affection at harvest.

Church Girl's first sinner friend

My mom thinks Natasha is a *Good Black*
because she lives in the tall orange houses
on 87th. What a conflicted color, orange.

Which came first, the color or the fruit?
Orange can't pick a side, claims the good
parts of red & yellow. A hybrid. The Good Blacks

worked for everything they have. Natasha's mom
reminds us we're *African-American* in her home.
Black describes a thing not people. Which came first,

the object or the color? Orange can't pick a side,
won't claim the bad parts of red & yellow. Her
parents remind us the N-word is ten times worse

when we say it. Their reasons aren't clear. They don't
explain themselves to children. The next time,
my mom drives up the twists & turns smiling.

Her daughter made a friend who lives *here.* Her child
of God can learn much from another closed off girl.
My moms says new houses use the orange brick.

Asks if I'm wearing clean socks. A house
like that needs shoes off. I try to think of other
important orange things when our moms meet.

Cones in the street stop car accidents.
My first school was by the Orange Line,
they bused all the black people in.

I meet my first boyfriend with Natasha at Tuley Park.
We dated for three unsupervised hours. Ran around
with him until my lips were cold & grey. My boyfriend & I

broke up when when it's time to walk back up
the hill. Natasha stops me from saying where
she lives. She grabs the paper from his hand

& lets the number swish to the ground like an abandoned
feather. At the end of the day, parts of the sunset are orange.
Natasha tells me I'm too friendly. Pulls out a five

for McDonalds she won't share & says
we're not like *them*. She pronounces
them like her mother. The outside world is full

of poor people. Can't go kissing them all.
My mom expects a full report the ride home.
I explain my wholesome & wealthy fun.

Tell her the carpet is white in the basement. They have
a TV in the kitchen & both cars fit in their garage. I leave
out my first kiss. My mom wants to know when

I'm going over Natasha's house again. She has school
tomorrow night, & the night after that. My mom gets
off work late & wants to drive straight to class.

Last night she fell asleep in all her clothes on the couch
& I tucked her in. I don't answer her question & lean
my head against the window. I notice the dashes in the road.

They're a bold orange & thrive separate.

After church she gets high again

After the repass the fun aunt goes home to rest. Her bed
is a lonely positive. A break before the celebration. A bottle
of confetti hums from the medicine cabinet. Music is vital
for a gathering. Downstairs, the rest of the family trails in
with full stomachs & puffed eyes. Death crowds homes

with relatives; uninvited grief carriers that won't cloud
their own homes with sadness. Later, we'll find what is left
of her pills. For now, she spins in the middle of our mourning
with stories about her past. She used to be in love. She used to be
pretty like her nieces & the photos shouting from the walls.

She snatches her frozen self off the hook & sways
with the frame in silence. *If we're blessed, we'll all die
old but ugly.* In the chapel my feet wouldn't go near
the casket. At her house, they tap on a beat
she thinks she hears. In a few months I get a call

the fun aunt is dead. Killed herself in search of another party
when she was sad. Died alone with confetti clogging her throat.
Coughed & the colors blocked her view. Her & the car,
an incomplete mosaic on the tree. I hang up the phone & return
to the concert. My heartbeat finds the music I swallowed.

I close my eyes & welcome splattered hues. At the beginning
of a high it's important to remind yourself you did this
to feel good. No bad news brings a pro down. I've trained
for this. I repeat my favorite colors over & over again until
I push to the front. Rambling & swaying through the songs

alone while my blood prepares for another funeral. Grateful it mixes with the hum of my pills. Grateful for the dance she taught me.

2015

there was the time me, her & him did the same drug
every two weeks. always at a different place. pushing
through clouds of friends who puffed on about *substance abuse*

while smoking their own cigarettes. the trick is to keep
moving. if I stop my mind settles. we don't want to sink.
being higher is a hurdle we can leap over. we already

have a great running start. the seventh stop this night
we're on a strangers roof considering the skyline. shouldn't
jump now. there are too many witnesses. can get

used to the pace if I'm rolling with friends. can stay
up if we keep running. I blinked and the sun was rising,
the panic warming me up. *why go back? we just left.* tonight

I watched myself from the balcony snatching the crumbs
from his palm with inch long nails. my hands, impatient
rakes scraping for the dose to keep me speeding. it's another

night stirred into the same night. I blinked and the sun
was rising. we're blurring down Lake Shore Drive arguing
who will abandon who first. she begged him not to drop

her off now. we need each other to come down or our whole
night washes away. I blinked and the sun was rising. never able
to cry if I'm alone. we knew the sadness creeping in is part

of the come down. we sit in a circle in the front
& say we're never doing this shit again. we don't promise.
can't feel like an addict if I'm always with my friends.

Come Thou Fount Hymn

An erasure

Come,   every blessing
Tune   sing   grace
                 , never ceasing
         songs of loudest praise
Teach me
         flaming tongues
Praise   , I'm fixed
         Thy redeeming love

Oh,   grace how great
Daily I'm constrained
         goodness
Bind my   heart
           Lord, I feel it
       leave   God I love
      my heart,   seal it
Seal it   above

On Job

When an event goes
wrong it is encouraged

to thank God anyway.
God makes no mistakes

is the string that keeps
me tied to him. What if

faith during hard times
is just a leash while I'm

a pawn in whatever
chest puffing

contest God has
with the Devil?

For Korah

*After Korah led a rebellion against Moses, God split the ground
open. Korah, his followers, their wives & children fell into the
Earth. God brought the ground back together & dropped fire from
the sky on the rest. The next day He gave the final rebels a plague.*

My Sunday School teacher thinks
we've forgotten God is a murderer.
Sometimes family & close friends
will betray God & then the earth can't
remember the last time it ate. Sometimes
God will make a flash decision. Ignore the cracks
in His plan & follow. God opened up the earth
& swallowed Moses' enemies. Smashed
the pieces of the broken ground together. Crushed
them like a pressed tulip in a forgotten book.
Then they became dirt. Helped the land be richer
& more fertile. Korah's blood fed the worms;
a little red sea of his own. Maybe one flower grows
yearly; a recurring tombstone & reminder.
Our God is the creator & the destroyer.
Our loyalty chooses the side the coin will land.
Poor Moses. Vouching for old friends was a waste.
An added spec in dirt, an overlooked splotch
in the ground. This lesson is the church's favorite
story. Reminds us Moses couldn't even save
someone from God's wrath. God's wrath
is only for those not saved. Save your words
for God's love. Save God's love for you
& only you.

I sleep next to ▮▮▮▮▮▮▮ after

and then he woke me up by snoring
commendable I was able to fall asleep
this is his bed now he is rooted I
am snapped hanging by splinters
commendable I was able to fall asleep
maybe it was the best defense after all I
am snapped hanging by splinters laying
next to him maybe it was the best
defense after all remembering roots can
hide their wicked in dirt laying next to
him above the ground remembering
roots can hide their wicked in dirt I
wish I only needed sunlight above the
ground pure, safe, recovered I wish I
only needed sunlight this is his bed
now he is rooted pure, safe, recovered,
and then he woke me up by snoring

Cut

I notice my hand is sliced
open after the broken mug is empty.
I am at home drinking leftover
liquor in shadows from the streetlight.
I forget who died this time. The rain
remembers. My mom taught me
to turn off the lights during storms.
I don't live with her anymore.
Still, my house is dark. Can barely
see the blood shaped smile spread
in my palm. It's comforting to
know I can still make myself laugh.
I close my fingers & try to
keep joy in my fist.

for Ginger Ale

When my stomach protested, my momma would bring ginger ale.
Without ice in the cup, she'd pray over bubbling ginger ale.

It's the medicine & the communion. The lone drink
& the chaser. You're balanced on that high-string ginger ale.

The only pop with a cure. Stir it with dark liquor. Lose
track of how much I am drinking with ginger ale.

Everyone around me is dying. Some on purpose, the rest
in scattered jolts. I need to mix you with something ginger ale.

Protect me from the hangover & when I'm sorry enough, food.
Tell my friends *I ate earlier.* My burp rings out ginger ale.

Settle & fill my belly for days. *Where have you been?* Alive,
sad, home with an upset stomach spewing ginger ale.

After church she gets high again

& let the church say

                        amen.

& let the church say

                        God will wipe you clean
                        from anything.

roll up his sleeves & grab me
out from the sewer. from all this
grime. God is the only one willing
to sift through me & pick out
the gold. to shove in my face-
of course. I can see how good
he's been to me, again.

                        Isn't he so forgiving?

I started praying again.

                        Aren't you so happy now?

I never think of myself as disloyal
until I'm reminded. He'll never
fully wash me clean. A spinning
lesson my niece can learn from.
Wring me out & hang me to dry. Saints
need to see who they're praying for.

                        you are sin. you are sad
                        because you are a sinner.
                        you are a sinner because
                        you are sad.

I sin & misery wanders
into my home. I get saved
& it never leaves.

My father misspeaks

and calls me the name of his dying sister.

I watch the name empty out. Every syllable

    removing herself from his mouth slowly.

    She expands between us, flooding the room

with her favorite flower. The photo chosen

for the obituary floats pass us. We stop talking

    behind her name to sit soggy in our grief. Waiting

    for the other to acknowledge the spill. I drove

for an hour to get here. My own siblings mortality

blaring through the speakers. The whole ride is

    grief practice. I sort through topics on the road

    that will lead us away from speaking about death.

I even bring up my lack of a ~~dating~~ life. Still, her

name finds a way to his mouth. I rehearsed this

    conversation but can't respond. Her name swelling

    in the silence. My own name dissolving in the quiet.

Jonah was trapped before he met the fish

Who knew after the first raindrop the storm was Jonah's
fault? I would have. Guilt has a smell that lingers

worse than the meat fishermen sift through daily. Anyone
with a long shadow dragging through the ground wouldn't

be welcomed aboard, especially someone whose only visible luggage
is the slump in his shoulders. I'd recognize that dip anywhere.

The storm bubbled over & Jonah dripped to the bottom
of the boat. Silent & low, praying everything above him would settle.

I time how long I can hold my breath underwater for 13 straight days.
Every evening I took an extra-large bottle of wine, filled the bathtub

& locked the door. *Maybe tonight will be the night
they find me.* Jonah hid like an untrained dog who wet the rug

when his owner came home too late. My roommate comes home
early, knocks to ask if I'm ok. I let my words leak out under the door.

They form a puddle of false relief. Is killing myself a sin if
I really want to die? Jonah, a man dull enough to think God can't

see him at all times. He sees when I dip my head back,
let the water reach my ears & keep going. Keep sinking.

A prophet disappearing gets God's attention. A depressed
twenty-something does not. *God would never follow me*

across an ocean, or my bathroom to change my mind. I am aware
I will never be loved as much. He only comes to sit on the edge

of the tub to hold the timer. My Lord, see how long can I hold
my breath? Once I broke my record. Opened my eyes under

the sea. Felt my feet push back & watched me float up on my own.
My nose & mouth forced above the surface to remember

what air was. God held Jonah underwater until he was his prophet
again. God saves my life while keeping his hands dry. I accomplish

nothing. My body doesn't let me. My God doesn't let me. God
might let me drown one day, if I practice hiding better. A

bigger tub & whiskey this time. An empty house & a nap below.
Is it even my body if I am made in his image?

Is it even a bath if God wants a baptism?

My Tribute Hymn

An erasure

      can I say thanks
For the things You have done for me?
      so undeserved
            to prove Your love for me;
    voices of   angels
Could not express
All that I   ever hope to be
I owe it all to Thee

To God
To God
To God be the glory
   the things He has done

With   blood He   saved me
With   power He   raised me;
To God be the glory
For the things

Just let me live
         Lord
   if I gain any praise
Let it go

To God
To God
To God be the glory
For the things He has done

Act Three

On Job

A footnote hangs beneath each blessing.
It lingers patiently under the swelled joy;

usually overlooked. Of course God won
the bet. He created all the competing factors.

The Devil was forbidden to kill Job. Even
if Job wanted to die, God protected him.

Some days faith feels like a faulty alarm
system. Am I'm only guarded by a thin curtain

of prayers? Some days faith is the only fabric
I can hold on to. I dig my nails in until it rips.

After church she gets high again

she isn't pure but   we still worship her

early today,   Sunday. still hope

she blesses us   after coming down

from her throne.   we pride ourselves in

being a loyal   following. rebuilt the

church after her   overdose. we remain in

prayer   until her resurrection.

Church Girl raps to herself under the covers

this is the year of insecurities / baptized in
impurities / pull glass out my knuckles / mirror

punching, gritting wisdom teeth / one day I'll love
myself / till then I'll burn it, third degree /

watching all I use to love / simmer right in front
of me / you ain't better than this / butterfly

pushed off a cliff / fumble through flying
instructions / wait for the ground to miss / I'm

bound to your ignorance / surrounded by your
fingerprints / eat insides on purpose / still

       regurgitate my innocence

I hate myself more than you do / sharpening my
loose screws / slide them in palms for /

handshakes when I greet you / a church-going
sinner, / feening, starving for every boost /

weak child of god / knows scriptures still won't
improve / on Sundays my mirror / slithers itself

back together / even the lines don't show / peel a
layer and pray better / hide my scales in long

skirts / tattoo my skin when I'm hurt / unraveling
at both ends / like all my Bible's leather

It wasn't all bad, I barely ever have stage fright now

I share the pulpit with the preachers. We all need
attention. My church family is my first audience.
They feel proud of their investment. I learn mic
control & stage presence before I learn why all
women here wear skirts. I never earned an answer.

One summer, I played Jesus. Dragged an invisible
cross down the aisle with drawn on thorns. I mimic
suffering & stumble in the same footsteps. I'm a
talented performer. The same summer I have a
meeting with my mom & a church leader

about my *inquisitive nature*. On the way home,
we practice a new song. My mom & I harmonize
driving down Garfield. She teaches me the role
of an alto is to support, stay low & follow. She
reminds me I don't have to perform for her love.

I mastered singing like her to be safe. Who am I
to go against God & the saints? My mom loves
every part of me. Her church doesn't. I learn
they need their faith in the alto key. They only
believe with their heads low to follow.

Thank you back parking lot

Janesha explains what sex is while I swing my legs
     on the peeling red bench. The paint chips stick
          to the back of my thighs like new skin.
     Her explanation is dead wrong but we both nod
& look away from each other.
Church girls pretend in front of their friends   the most.
     The final amen escapes from the window
         above our heads but we don't look up.
     We burn in the sun where we belong.
Service is over. There's another one soon.

    //

        I love this parking lot;
        my first playground.
        The cracks in the asphalt
        near the back fence mark
        the section for Four Square.
        Junie has a corner store
        in her trunk for the children
        who can't go out the gate.
        Janesha unbraids her rope
        & we claim the territory
        in front of the shed.
        Church mothers remind us
        to hold our chests when
        we jump & refasten
        the barrettes that fly off
        our braids. They scold girls
        showing their knees

while their colorful,
wide-brimmed hats
hit each other.

//

I wish every part of this church was the back parking lot.

The only place God won't divide us.

Where else can I learn the Juke Slide in lace socks and church shoes?

Where else can I fight Marie & pray she gets home safely?

//

I want the back parking lot.

I want the snow cones my cousin sold under the air
conditioner & the dance parties on the side of the garage.
I want the dares, the flying footballs & double-dutch
competitions. I want to stay outside until our moms
pretend to leave us. I want to lean against the shed &
gripe about my unpierced ears. I want to push Shay
for suggesting we try what they did on Parent Trap.

I need my community.

If only I could snatch the back parking lot up
& stuff it under my shirt. I know stealing is a sin
but so is loneliness.

Church Girl learns to pray again

For Chase

I dread when the food comes
at the restaurant. My family prays

over each meal. The saints' routine
is embarrassing. I keep my eyes

open when my dad starts. My secret
act of resistance. We pray during all

car rides. I watch the world go by out
the window. We pray on the edge

of my bed before we sleep. I
still get a nightmare. My parents pray

to remind God they're still there. I
stay quiet & hope God forgets me.

//

God prefers to listen to
His saint over her daughter.
I beg my mom to pray for me
while I'm high. Everything is

a punishment. I understand
what I did wrong. The
worse type of sinner is
the sinner who knows

better. I tell her I'll come to church.
My mom offers to come to my house
instead. I put her on speaker,
stay quiet & hope God forgets me.

//

His house is a sanctuary I've invaded
for a week. When I'm away from him
      he prays for my safety.

I stay here to save his breath. The worse
type of sinner is the sinner who knows
      better. I'm a heathen falling

in love with a soul I don't deserve. In the
morning, he rests his hand on my head
      while I pretend to be sleep.

I hear him pray for me in the silence.
I stay quiet & hope God forgives me.

//

Our kitchen is small. We smash
into each other like we're trying
to merge the skills our mom's
taught us to survive. This apartment
is our ragged kingdom. We play
It while taping the windows in
the winter & platonically shower
to maximize hot water. We pray
over our dinner before we eat, a

recent routine I didn't know
I missed. I'm out of practice. We
learned to thank God before asking
for a favor. He thanks God for the
roof over our heads & the hands that made
the food, my hands. I peek at him during
his prayer to make sure he means me.
The wrinkle in between his eyebrows
makes a cross.

//

I practice praying while he snores in my ear.

His sighs are my cheat code. God must have

a soft spot for me. I'm not dead yet. I perfect

my *amen* to close out future prayers. I nudge

him to roll on his side & soften his breathing.

He reaches out to hold me without opening

an eye. *Thank you God, amen* I whisper. How

can I claim God doesn't listen to sinners?

How else could I get such a blessing?

It is written!

Genesis 29:17- Leah was tender eyed; but Rachel was beautiful and well favored.

Even the Bible knows I'm fine. Look
it up yourself. The story is the same;
in all versions I'm a hit. Jacob worked
14 years for Rachel so I know shorty was
a head turner. Might have to peruse the
Good Book more often. I'm done sitting
through sermons that remind me I'll burn
soon; never quick enough. Today, the Word™
shouts me out. Finally! An affirmation crawling
under the attacks. I hear your message loud
& clear God! I'm a dime that is indeed top
of the line. Your prophet wrote I'm beautiful.
I'm even well favored. Is her name pronounced
Lee-ah or Lay-ah? I don't remember. The
first half of the scripture is honestly boring
but the second half is a masterpiece.

Acknowledgements

Huge love & much gratitude to the publications that accepted poems from this collection, some in different forms.

The Shallow Ends "Church Girl sings for the congregation"
The Rumpus "I sleep next to ▮▮▮▮▮▮▮ after"
Poetry Magazine "For the black girl who doesn't know how to braid hair."
Washington Square Review "Jonah was trapped before he met the fish"

Massive thank you to Button Poetry for publishing my first collection.

Thank you to all the people who read the early drafts. You helped me make a book out of rants. Fatimah Asghar, Hanif Abdurraqib, Kevin Coval, Brittany Rogers, & Toaster.

Thank you Hector Padilla for creating amazing cover art from my words.

I write this for all the church babies. Special thank you to my Church Baby Crew that wandered 47th with me, taught me rope & let me be weird. Gabby, Regina, Neromi, April, Shanaya, Khalilah, Tatiana, Ashanti, Ariel, Nikki, Jasmine, Joi, & Deanna. You held my secrets & were my first friends.

Thank you to Brittany Jones, Darius Montague & Unique Love. You made DePaul a home & kept me safe.

Thank you to my all family I met through art. Thank you for reading my poems. Thank you for sharing my poems & thank you for booking me. Thank you for coming to my first shows or sliding my broke ass on the list to yours. Thank you for listening to me cry & checking me when I doubted myself. Britteney Black Rose Kapri, Dimress Dunnigan, Fatimah Warner, Qurissy Lopez, Cristela Rodriguez, Sarah Bruno, Kaina Castillo, Dominique James, Kush Thompson, Dominique Chestand, Cydney Edwards, Jasmine Barber, Reese Amaru, Adam Levin, Molly Kuhlman, Aris Theotokatos, Sen Morimoto, Eddie Sikazwe, Jeff Badu, Emon Lauren, Patricia Fraizer, Kara Jackson, Matt Muse, Lisandra Bernadett, José Olivarez, Kai Davis, Jamila Woods, Hieu Nguyen, Safia Elhillo, Danez Smith, Franny Choi, Paul Tran, Nate Marshall, Olivia Gatwood, Ashlee Haze, Lyric, Oompa, Porsha Olayiwola, Bernard Ferguson, Simone Beaubien, Eloisa Amezcua, J. David, Avery R. Young, Robbie Q Telfer, Krista Franklin, Diamond Sharp, Eve Ewing, Rachel McKibbens, Rachel Wiley, Ajané Dawkins, Davon Clark, Nick Ward, Xandria Phillips, Benjamin Williams, Kee Stein, Maceo Haymes, Billy Tuggle, Josh Fleming, Luis Carranza, Morelia Rodriguez, Ken Muñoz, Sammy Ortega, Jalen Kobayashi, TLC, Mercedes Zapata, Karla Gutierrez, Gabriela Ibarra, Kane One, Sllime, Joseph Chilliams, Saba, Melo, Frsh, Squeak, Dae Dae, Nachelle Pugh, John, Mausi, Marguerite Meyer, André Schürmann, Aline Pieth & Urs Hofer. Thank you to all my LTAB family, Pink Door kin & anyone who has come to a Big Kid Slam.

Thank you Chase.

Thank you to my teacher friends & mentors who love their students unconditionally. Who supported me during those five years teaching in Chicago Public Schools. Malika Jackson, Erica Taylor, Mariah Newsome, Brock Massie, Patricia Razo, Adam Jimenez, Kevin Farrell, Kierston Castleberry, Teacher King, Principal King, Katy Adler, Jessie Macadoo, Brenda Shiller, Amber Szuch, Diego Moore & Shauna Brooks.

Thank you to my mom & dad for proving love is an action word. For allowing me to make my own decisions & for loving me the same. Thank you to my brothers Adriane & William. Thank you to my favorite cousin Kevin & my entire family: the Jacksons, the Davis', & the Harris'.

Thank you reader & Thank you God.

Rachel "Raych" Jackson is a writer, educator and performer. While teaching third grade in Chicago Public Schools, Jackson competed on numerous national poetry teams and individual competitions. She is the 2017 NUPIC Champion and a 2017 Pink Door fellow. Jackson recently voiced 'DJ Raych' in the game *Mad Verse City*. Her latest play, "Emotions & Bots", premiered at the Woerdz Festival in Lucerne, Switzerland. She co-created and co-hosts *Big Kid Slam*, a monthly poetry show in Chicago. Jackson's work has been published by many—including *Poetry Magazine, The Rumpus, The Shallow Ends, and Washington Square Review*. She currently lives in Chicago.

www.RaychJackson.com
Twitter: @RaychJackson
Instagram: @RaychJackson

Other Books by Button Poetry

If you enjoyed this book, please consider checking out some of our others, below. Readers like you allow us to keep broadcasting and publishing. Thank you!

Neil Hilborn, *Our Numbered Days*
Hanif Abdurraqib, *The Crown Ain't Worth Much*
Olivia Gatwood, *New American Best Friend*
Donte Collins, *Autopsy*
Melissa Lozada-Oliva, *peluda*
Sabrina Benaim, *Depression & Other Magic Tricks*
William Evans, *Still Can't Do My Daughter's Hair*
Rudy Francisco, *Helium*
Guante, *A Love Song, A Death Rattle, A Battle Cry*
Rachel Wiley, *Nothing Is Okay*
Neil Hilborn, *The Future*
Phil Kaye, *Date & Time*
Andrea Gibson, *Lord of the Butterflies*
Blythe Baird, *If My Body Could Speak*
Desireé Dallagiacomo, *SINK*
Dave Harris, *Patricide*
Michael Lee, *The Only Worlds We Know*

Available at buttonpoetry.com/shop and more!